ALTERNATOR BOOKS™

INCREDIBLE ANIMAL TRIVIA

FUN FACTS AND QUIZZES

Eric Braun

Lerner Publications ◆ Minneapolis

Lerner Publications Company
A division of Lerner Publishing Group, Inc.
241 First Avenue North
Minneapolis, MN 55401 USA

For reading levels and more information, look up this title at www.lernerbooks.com.

Main body text set in Aptifer Slab LT Pro Regular.
Typeface provided by Linotype AG.

Library of Congress Cataloging-in-Publication Data

The Cataloging-in-Publication Data for *Incredible Animal Trivia: Fun Facts and Quizzes* is on file at the Library of Congress.
ISBN 978-1-5124-8330-7 (lib. bdg.)
ISBN 978-1-5124-8335-2 (eb pdf)

Manufactured in the United States of America
1-43337-33157-8/23/2017

CONTENTS

FASTER, FASTER!

Mountain goats are one of the hardest animals to catch. Why? They're the animal world's fastest rock climbers and can jump 12 feet (4 m) to avoid predators.

Q. Guess who's faster—an adult human or an adult hippo?

A. A fully grown hippopotamus can outrun a person!

A mite—a tiny, spiderlike creature—has been recorded running at up to 322 body lengths per second. For a person, that would be like running 1,300 miles (2,092 km) per hour!

A cheetah can sprint more than 70 miles (113 km) per hour. But if it runs that fast for more than thirty seconds, something bad can happen. Can you guess what?

A. It can suffer brain damage.
B. It can break its legs.
C. It can have a heart attack.
D. It throws up.

The answer is A, brain damage. Now *that* is fast.

Q. **The peregrine falcon reaches nearly 200 miles (322 km) per hour when it dives through the air. But Brazilian free-tailed bats are the fastest horizontal fliers. How fast do you think they fly?**

A. **Brazilian free-tailed bats can hit 100 miles (161 km) per hour!**

A species of Australian tiger beetle can run faster than any other insect—about 5.6 miles (9 km) per hour. But when it runs at top speed, its eyes stop working. It has to slow down to see again.

The second-fastest marine animal is the killer whale, which can swim at speeds up to 34.5 miles (55.5 km) per hour. Which animal is faster?

A. The octopus
B. The tiger shark
C. The sailfish
D. Plankton

It's C, the sailfish. This fish increases its speed by leaping out of the water. Sailfish can swim an amazing 68 miles (109 km) per hour.

The Moroccan flic-flac spider cartwheels itself away from dangerous situations. This unusual motion allows it to travel at up to 6.5 feet (2 m) per second.

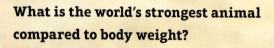

SUPERSTRENGTH

What is the world's strongest animal compared to body weight?

A. The elephant
B. The hummingbird
C. The dung beetle
D. The great white shark

The answer is the dung beetle. This tiny insect can pull 1,141 times its own body weight. That's like a human pulling six double-decker buses full of people.

The ostrich's knees bend backward, and it can kick forward with 2,000 pounds of pressure per square inch (141 kg per sq. cm). That's strong enough to kill a lion with one kick.

Q. How strong is a gorilla?

A. A gorilla can lift ten times its body weight— that's about the weight of thirty humans!

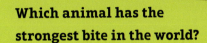

Which animal has the strongest bite in the world?

A. The lion
B. The Nile crocodile
C. The mosquito
D. The great white shark

The answer is B.

Geckos have a powerful grip that allows them to climb even the smoothest walls and ceilings. Each foot is strong enough to grip with the force of twenty times the animal's body weight.

The harpy eagle is believed to be the most powerful eagle in the world. These massive raptors have talons the size of grizzly bear claws, and here's the truly scary part: Their grasp can easily puncture the skulls of their prey. Their talons have more crushing power than a wolf's bite.

7

FIERCE AND FEISTY

Tomato frogs make a glue that can make their enemies' lips stick together. Did you think a frog could be so sneaky?

The Komodo dragon, largest of all lizards, can reach 10 feet (3 m) long and 250 pounds (113 kg). And it is not only large. It has a venomous bite. Which of the following is also true of these terrifying beasts?

A. They are known to prey on humans.
B. They can jump 20 feet (6 m) in the air.
C. They can run nearly as fast as a cheetah.
D. Their claws are as sharp as razor blades.

If you find yourself in the wild in Indonesia, where Komodo dragons live, watch out—the answer is A!

Mind Blown:

Q. Which mammal do you think has the most teeth?

A. Can you believe it's the dolphin? Some dolphins have up to 250 teeth.

Q. How do you think the bullet ant—native to Central and South America—got its name?

A. The name *bullet ant* comes from the power of its sting. Victims say it feels as if they've been shot.

In 1998 fifty-six thousand salmon were killed in half an hour in New Zealand. Something attacked the fish. What do you think it was?

A. A swarm of disease-carrying mosquitoes
B. Fishers with wide nets and bait
C. A swarm of jellyfish
D. A school of piranha

The answer is C, jellyfish!

The black mamba snake has one of the world's most toxic bites. A human who is bitten by a black mamba can lose consciousness in an hour.

HIDDEN AWAY

Alone in a hole: Pink fairy armadillos—the smallest of all types of armadillos at about 5 to 6 inches (13 to 15 cm) long—dig deep holes and burrow by themselves for most of their lives. They usually come out only at night to find ants and plants to eat.

Watch your step: The horned adder, a venomous snake that lives in southern Africa, uses a swimming motion to bury itself in the sand.

Flex those muscles: To avoid predators, octopuses, squids, and cuttlefish can change color to match their environment. Some can turn up to fifty different colors! How do they do it? They use special muscles to control pigment cells in their skin.

Dig deep: Geoducks are a type of clam that bury themselves deep in the sand. They can live like this for more than one hundred years!

Walking sticks: Don't be surprised if you see a stick strolling your way. Stick insects can hide in plain sight because they look almost exactly like a twig or stick.

What a lovely flower . . . or not: Some praying mantises look exactly like the flowers they live on. This helps them make surprise attacks on their prey.

Underground mansions: Naked mole rats live underground in colonies of as many as two hundred members. They work together to create tunnels and rooms underground in areas as large as six football fields!

ODD ACTIONS

Sea otters hold hands when they sleep. That way they don't drift apart.

How do tarantulas fight off predators?

A. They don't have any predators.
B. They tear out their hair.
C. They spit venom.
D. They roll into a ball.

The answer is B—they tear out their hair and throw it at their enemies. The hair is sticky and slows down predators, especially if it gets into their eyes.

One species of jellyfish, the *Turritopsis dohrnii*, can live forever! Adults can transform back into babies and grow up all over again.

The kakapo is the only parrot that doesn't fly. Instead, a kakapo uses its strong legs to climb trees.

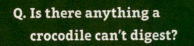

Q. Is there anything a crocodile can't digest?

A. Yep—rocks. A crocodile's stomach can break down a turtle's shell, but it can't break down rocks. But that's OK. Crocodiles eat rocks anyway, and it doesn't hurt them.

The males in a cheetah family stick together for their whole lives. But the females avoid one another and live solitary lives.

Can you guess what koalas do when they feel too hot?

A. They hug a tree to cool down.
B. They jump out of a tree to feel the breeze.
C. They lick one another.
D. They go for a swim.

It might sound crazy, but these cuties hug trees to chill.

Tapirs look like pigs with trunks. Just like elephants, they use their trunks to grab branches and fruit. They can even use their trunks like snorkels if they go underwater!

Anole lizards do push-ups to threaten other lizards.

HOW BIG IS IT?

What's the world's smallest bird?

A. The flea parrot
B. The needle-billed finch
C. The speck tern
D. The bee hummingbird

The answer is D, the bee hummingbird. It's about the size of a bee and the weight of a penny. (Those other answers aren't even real birds.)

Think you know what jellyfish look like? Think about this: Almost all jellyfish (about 90 percent) are smaller than a human thumbnail.

Mind Blown:
A frog in South America grows backward! It can reach 11 inches (27 cm) as a tadpole but shrinks to no larger than 1.5 inches (4 cm) as an adult frog.

Q. What's the biggest snake in the world?

A. Anacondas—they can eat animals as large as deer or even crocodiles!

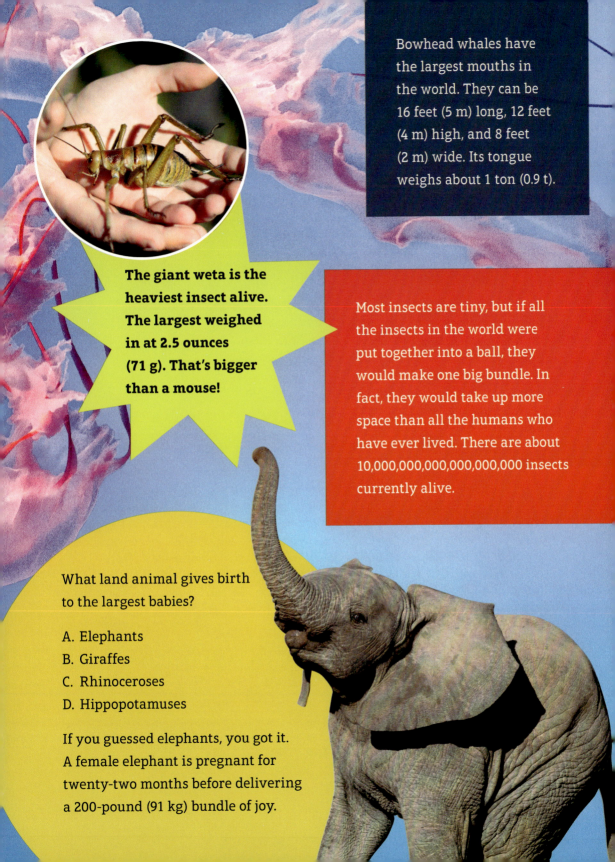

Bowhead whales have the largest mouths in the world. They can be 16 feet (5 m) long, 12 feet (4 m) high, and 8 feet (2 m) wide. Its tongue weighs about 1 ton (0.9 t).

The giant weta is the heaviest insect alive. The largest weighed in at 2.5 ounces (71 g). That's bigger than a mouse!

Most insects are tiny, but if all the insects in the world were put together into a ball, they would make one big bundle. In fact, they would take up more space than all the humans who have ever lived. There are about 10,000,000,000,000,000,000 insects currently alive.

What land animal gives birth to the largest babies?

A. Elephants
B. Giraffes
C. Rhinoceroses
D. Hippopotamuses

If you guessed elephants, you got it. A female elephant is pregnant for twenty-two months before delivering a 200-pound (91 kg) bundle of joy.

UNDER THE SEA

Octopuses are supersmart! In fact, each of an octopus's arms can think and act independently. That means each arm can solve different problems at the same time—as if each arm has its own brain.

How many eyes does a scallop have?

A. None
B. 2
C. 50
D. 100

Believe it or not, these tiny shellfish can have up to one hundred eyes!

Sharkskin is made up of denticles—basically, tiny scales facing toward its tail—that make water flow past extra smoothly. A designer created racing swimsuits modeled after sharkskin, but they allowed their wearers to move so quickly through water that the suits were banned from competition!

Killifish live in puddles in roads—and they somehow don't get hurt when car tires crash into the puddle! Killifish also jump from puddle to puddle when the puddle they are in is drying out.

An endangered fish in Australia has fins that look like hands. It is known as a handfish. The fish can swim, but it usually walks along the seabed using its fins instead.

Herring sometimes gather in huge schools of hundreds of millions of fish. These massive groups can stretch for many miles and are believed to be the world's biggest animal grouping.

Manatees can rise and sink in the water without appearing to move a muscle. How do you think they do it?

A. Their fat takes in faint electrical vibrations from the water.
B. They fart.
C. The moon's gravitational pull influences them because they're so big.
D. They use sound.

It may sound incredible, but the answer is B!

HIGH IN THE SKY

The gannet is a seabird that hunts for fish by diving into the water, just like many other seabirds. But the gannet hits the water at 90 miles (145 km) per hour! It has an extrathick skull and special sacs of air built into its neck to protect it when it hits the water.

Q. Do insects flap their wings?

A. Nope. Instead, insect wings vibrate.

Dragonflies have four wings and can fly forward, backward, and sideways, and they can make sudden sharp changes in direction. They can even hover.

When bats are flying, they breathe two hundred times a minute . . . compared to ten times an hour when they're hibernating.

In 2007 a female shorebird called a bar-tailed godwit set a world record for the longest measured nonstop flight. It flew all the way from Alaska to New Zealand. That's 7,145 miles (11,500 km)!

The Sunda colugo—also known as a flying lemur—doesn't actually fly. But it does leap quickly from treetop to treetop, so it looks as if it is flying.

Military and law enforcement officers in some countries are training golden eagles to attack drones.

Rüppell's griffon vultures are the highest-flying birds in the world. Can you guess how high they can fly?

A. 1,000 feet (305 m)
B. 10,000 feet (3,048 m)
C. 37,000 feet (11,278 m)
D. 47,000 feet (14,326 m)

The answer is C—37,000 feet. One vulture is known to have crashed into an airplane while flying that high.

INCREDIBLE INTELLIGENCE

If they know another bird is watching, **ravens** will pretend to hide their food in one place while secretly hiding it somewhere else.

Skipper caterpillars fling their poop far away to confuse predators.

Bees can recognize human faces.

Pigs can learn to play video games that are too hard for three-year-old humans to play.

Chimpanzees can learn sign language—and use it to communicate with other chimps.

Octopuses are hard to keep as pets because they're so good at escaping from aquariums.

Some **macaque monkeys** have learned to use coins to buy snacks from vending machines.

Dolphins have names for one another—they call to one another using specific whistles.

THAT'S DISGUSTING!

Talk about a tight fit! When Darwin's frogs are tadpoles, they live in their fathers' vocal sacs. Dad coughs them up when they're fully formed frogs.

Think you're stressed? An octopus can become *really* stressed if it's not well taken care of. It can get so stressed out that it

A. Eats its own arms
B. Squirts ink involuntarily
C. Throws itself on the beach and dies
D. Snaps at other octopuses

The answer is A. It eats its own arms.

Camels have urine that's as thick as maple syrup. To survive in the desert, their bodies need to absorb as much water as possible before getting rid of waste.

The world's largest leech is the giant Amazon leech. It can grow up to 18 inches (46 cm). That's a lot of bloodsucking power!

When the wild markhor goat of central Asia chews, a foamlike substance drops out of its mouth. Local people, who believe the substance can help cure people bitten by poisonous snakes, collect the dried goo.

Before there were refrigerators, people in Russia and Finland placed live frogs in their milk to keep it fresh.

Can you guess what mother koalas feed their newborn joeys?

A. Mineral-rich mud
B. Worms
C. Feces
D. Toe jam

If you guessed feces—or poop— great job! They need the bacteria in the feces to help them digest the leaves they'll eat when they're older.

The Fitzroy River turtle can breathe through its mouth or absorb oxygen from the water through its rear end. It's easier for the turtle to breathe through its rear end—especially during underwater hibernation.

ENDANGERED AND EXTINCT

How can you tell the age a mammoth was when it died?

A. Count its teeth.

B. Count the rings in its tusks.

C. Count its birthday candles.

D. Weigh its skull.

It's B—count the rings in its tusks.

Four million years ago, rodents the size of bulls lived in South America. Aren't you glad you didn't live then?

Q. What's the largest animal that ever walked on Earth?

A. A titanosaur—a sauropod dinosaur discovered in South America. It was nearly 120 feet (37 m) long and weighed 77 tons (70 t). That's as much as fifteen African elephants!

Irrawaddy dolphins in Southeast Asia sometimes help fishers by herding fish toward nets. But the dolphins are in danger of becoming extinct.

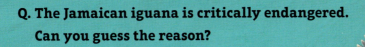

Q. The Jamaican iguana is critically endangered. Can you guess the reason?

A. The government introduced the mongoose to Jamaica to control its rat problem. But the mongoose didn't eat only rats—it also feasted on Jamaican iguana eggs.

The solenodon is the only mammal to inject venom through its teeth. It has been on Earth since the time of dinosaurs, but it is in danger of going extinct.

The cui-ui, a fish that lives in Nevada's Pyramid Lake, was thought to be extinct in the 1930s. But it has reappeared. How long do you think this fish can live?

A. 9 years
B. 16 years
C. 40 years
D. 100 years

The answer is C, forty years. That's one old fish!

Which of the following is *not* true about the endangered leatherback turtle?

A. It is the largest turtle in the world.
B. Its population is seriously decreasing due to humans collecting its eggs.
C. Its shell is flexible and rubbery.
D. It glows in the dark.

The answer is D. Leatherback turtles do not glow in the dark.

POPULAR PETS

Some hamsters can store half their weight in food in their cheeks.

Q. How many dogs are in the world?

A. There are nearly one billion dogs in the world.

A parakeet named Puck had the largest-ever vocabulary for a parrot. He knew 1,728 words!

Bearded dragons are popular pets. In 2005 researchers found something surprising. What do you think it was?

A. Bearded dragons can breathe fire.

B. Bearded dragons can regrow body parts.

C. Bearded dragons produce venom.

D. Bearded dragons should live only in Australia.

The answer is C. But don't worry, the venom is harmless for humans.

Which of these things is *not* true?

A. Dogs' nose prints are all unique, just like our fingerprints.
B. Dogs can smell your emotions.
C. The moisture on dogs' noses helps capture scents.
D. Some dogs have four nostrils.

It's D—but four nostrils would be pretty cool!

Mind Blown:
While guinea pigs are considered cute pets in many parts of the world, they are a delicacy in Peru. People there eat sixty-five million of them a year.

The deathstalker scorpion, featuring the worst sting of any scorpion worldwide, is a popular pet choice. Just don't rub its belly!

House cats are the only species of cat that can walk with its tail straight up in the air.

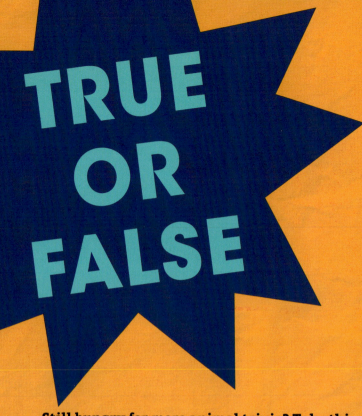

TRUE OR FALSE

Still hungry for more animal trivia? Take this short quiz to see how well you can spot a true trivia fact. You can find the answers on the next page.

1. A calico cat in Texas learned to ride a bike.

2. Ancient Greeks used stingray venom to numb pain.

3. A group of wombats is called a wisdom.

4. Orangutans suckle, or drink milk, from their mothers for their first six or seven years of life.

5. Researchers in Canada discovered fossils of a 508-million-year-old sea monster with fifty legs, giant claws, and a tentlike shell.

6. Scientists named a new species of ant a Radiohead, after the band of the same name.

7. Pigs don't sweat.

8. Seahorse partners sometimes "hold tails"—sort of like how people hold hands.

9. Eagles screech just because it feels so good to be flying.

10. Humans have more hair follicles than chimpanzees.

1) False. 2) True. 3) False. Most wombats do not form groups in the wild. 4) True. 5) True. 6) True. 7) True. 8) True. 9) False. They probably scream to warn predators to stay away. 10) False. They have the same number of hair follicles. Human hair is just much thinner, so it seems as if there is less of it.

WHO KNEW!?

Just can't get enough trivia? Here are some fun facts about trivia itself!

- The game Trivial Pursuit, which came out in 1981, has had many editions and has sold more than one hundred million copies. It has been turned into a TV show and several different kinds of video games.

- Every summer, trivia lovers from around the world get together in Las Vegas, Nevada, for the annual Trivia Championships of North America.

- In the 1950s, quiz shows were very popular on TV. But many shows rigged the outcome by giving some contestants answers, so people didn't enjoy watching the shows as much anymore.

- In 1966 the first published book of trivia came out. The book was called *Trivia*.

- The smallest amount won by a champion on the trivia game show *Jeopardy!* was one dollar.

FURTHER INFORMATION

Animal Planet: Wild Animals
http://www.animalplanet.com/wild-animals

BBC Nature: Animals
http://www.bbc.co.uk/nature/animals

Buckley, James, Jr. *Animals: A Visual Encyclopedia.* New York: Liberty Street, 2015.

National Geographic. *Animal Encyclopedia: 2,500 Animals with Photos, Maps, and More!* Washington, DC: National Geographic, 2012.

National Geographic Kids: Animals
http://kids.nationalgeographic.com/animals

Williams, Rachel, and Emily Hawkins. *Atlas of Animal Adventures: A Collection of Nature's Most Unmissable Events, Epic Migrations, and Extraordinary Behaviors.* New York: Wide Eyed, 2016.

PHOTO ACKNOWLEDGMENTS

The images in this book are used with the permission of: iStock.com/bmarshall1988, pp. 4–5 (background); iStock.com/zokru, p. 4; iStock.com/ca2hill, p. 5; iStock.com/vendys, pp. 6–7 (background); iStock.com/JohnCarnemolla, p. 6; iStock.com/SteveAllenPhoto, p. 7 (top); Wang LiQiang/Shutterstock.com, p. 7 (bottom); iStock.com/GlobalP, pp. 8–9 (center); iStock.com/bennymarty, p. 9 (top); iStock.com/reptiles4all, p. 9 (bottom); Nicholas Smythe/Science Source/Getty Images, p. 10 (top); Dario Sabljak/Shutterstock.com, p. 10 (bottom); iStock.com/Jonathan Austin Daniels, p. 11 (top); Vince Adam/Shutterstock.com, p. 11 (bottom); iStock.com/RobertDowner, pp. 12–13 (background); iStock.com/kugelblitz, p. 12 (top); Chris Birmingham/Wikimedia Commons (CC BY 2.0), p. 12 (bottom); iStock.com/Warmlight, p. 13; iStock.com/barbaraaaa, pp. 14–15 (background); iStock.com/cellistka, p. 14; Dinobass/Wikimedia Commons (CC BY-SA 4.0), p. 15 (top); iStock.com/Francois6, p. 15 (bottom); iStock.com/wrangel, pp. 16–17 (background); iStock.com/Mirko_Rosenau, p. 16; iStock.com/Andrea Izzotti, p. 17; Mmo iwdg/Wikimedia Commons (CC BY-SA 3.0), pp. 18–19 (background); iStock.com/MirekKijewski, p. 18 (top); iStock.com/caughtinthe, p. 18 (bottom); Vincent St. Thomas/Shutterstock.com, p. 19 (top); iStock.com/StuPorts, p. 19 (bottom); iStock.com/Wildnerdpix, p. 20 (top); iStock.com/akova, p. 20 (bottom); iStock.com/USO, p. 21 (top); iStock.com/Tashka, p. 21 (bottom); iStock.com/ZambeziShark, pp. 22–23 (background); Nature Picture Library/Alamy Stock Photo, p. 22; iStock.com/Nkarol, p. 23; iStock.com/aleks1949, pp. 24–25 (center); Isuaneye/Shutterstock.com, p. 24 (bottom); © Robin Winkelman/Dreamstime.com, p. 25 (top); James A Hancock/Science Source/Getty Images, p. 25 (bottom); iStock.com/Birute, pp. 26–27 (background); iStock.com/averess, p. 26; iStock.com/BIMKA1, p. 27 (top); Protasov AN/Shutterstock.com, p. 27 (bottom). Design elements: R-studio/Shutterstock.com; balabolka/Shutterstock.com.

Front cover: Wang LiQiang/Shutterstock.com (hummingbird); Gubin Yury/Shutterstock.com (hippopotamus); Gunnar Pippel/Shutterstock.com (goldfish); Eric Isselee/Shutterstock.com (chimpanzee); Panuwach/Shutterstock.com (animal doodles).